¡Felices fiestas! / Happy Holidays!

¡FELIZ DÍA DE SAN VALENTÍN!/ HAPPY VALENTINE'S DAY!

By Alex Appleby
Traducción al español: Christina Green

Gareth Stevens Publishing

Please visit our website, www.garethstevens.com. For a free color catalog of all our high-quality books, call toll free 1-800-542-2595 or fax 1-877-542-2596.

Library of Congress Cataloging-in-Publication Data

Appleby, Alex.
Happy Valentine's Day! = ¡Feliz día de San Valentín! / by Alex Appleby.
p. cm. — (Happy holidays! = ¡Felices fiestas!)
Parallel title: ¡Felices fiestas!
In English and Spanish.
Includes index.
ISBN 978-1-4339-9970-3 (library binding)
1. Valentine's Day — Juvenile literature. I. Appleby, Alex.II. Title.
GT4925.A66 2014
394.2618—d23

First Edition

Published in 2014 by
Gareth Stevens Publishing
111 East 14th Street, Suite 349
New York, NY 10003

Editor: Ryan Nagelhout
Designer: Sarah Liddell
Spanish Translation: Christina Green

Photo credits: Cover, p. 1 OlegDoroshin/Shutterstock.com; p. 5 © iStockphoto.com/ssj414; p. 7 © iStockphoto.com/fotostorm; pp. 9, 24 (hearts) © iStockphoto.com/nkbimages; p. 11 © iStockphoto.com/kirin_photo; pp. 13, 24 (valentines) auleena/Shutterstock.com; p. 15 Digital Vision/Thinkstock.com; p. 17 jsmith/E+/Getty Images; p. 19 © iStockphoto.com/Imagesbybarbara; pp. 21, 24 (roses) wjarek/Shutterstock.com; p. 23 © iStockphoto.com/Zorah.

Printed in the United States of America

CPSIA compliance information: Batch #CW14GS: For further information contact Gareth Stevens, New York, New York at 1-800-542-2595.

Contenido

Contents

El Día de San Valentín
es una fiesta divertida.

Valentine's Day
is a fun holiday.

BE
MINE

Es el 14 de febrero.

It is on February 14.

¡Es la fiesta del amor!

It is a holiday
about love!

I LOVE
YOU!

Damos regalos.

We give gifts to people.

Las personas
dan tarjetas
de San Valentín.

People give out cards.
These are valentines.

MINE
LOVE
happy valentine's day
LOVE
LOVE ME
YOU ARE MY
TODAY

Muchas tarjetas tienen forma de corazón.

Many cards look like little hearts.

Algunas personas
regalan flores.

Some people
give flowers.

Muchas personas reciben rosas.

Many people get roses.

¡Las rosas rojas significan amor!

Red roses mean love!

¡Las rosas azules representan amistad!

Blue roses are for friends!

Palabras que debes saber/ Words to Know

(los) corazones/ hearts

(las) rosas/ roses

(las) tarjetas de San Valentín/ valentines

Índice/Index